Already the W

Wick Poetry First Book Series

MAGGIE ANDERSON, EDITOR

Already the World
Victoria Redel GERALD STERN, JUDGE

Already
the
World

Poems by
Victoria Redel

For Laura —
Keep following the
dream of words
and heart —
Victoria Redel

The Kent State
University Press
Kent, Ohio, &
London, England

© 1995 by Victoria Redel
All rights reserved
Library of Congress Catalog Card Number 95-4151
ISBN 0-87338-530-6 (cloth)
ISBN 0-87338-531-4 (pbk.)
Manufactured in the United States of America

06 05 04 03 02   5 4 3 2

Library of Congress Cataloging-in-Publication Data

Redel, Victoria.
Already the world   :   by Victoria Redel.
p.   cm. — (Wick poetry first book series)
ISBN 0-87338-530-6 (cloth) — ISBN 0-87338-531-4 (pbk.) ∞
I. Title. II. Series.
PS3568.E3443A58   1995
811'.54—dc20   95-4151

British Library Cataloging-in-Publication data are available.

For my mother, Natasha.

CONTENTS

CONTENTS

III

ACKNOWLEDGMENTS

These poems first appeared in the following magazines and journals and are reprinted with permission: "At War," *Bomb Magazine;* "Talk the Big Hand Down," *Field;* "The Player" (appeared as "That Summer, New York"), *The New England Review;* "While the Baby Slept," *Provincetown Arts;* "The Way Hagar Tells It," *The Peaked Hills;* "On the Table," "Survivor," "Third Month," and "Ninth Month," *The Quarterly;* "Maybe There is Nothing Special Going On," "Calling Brother," and "Talking Angel," *Shankpainter;* "How the First Generation Learns," *The Seattle Review;* "Press," *Poetry Northwest.*

"Some Crazy Dancing" was awarded the 1987 Chester H. Jones Award.

All thanks, all gratitude, all praise to Maggie Anderson, Richard Corum, Stanley Kunitz, Gordon Lish, and Gerald Stern. And more thanks to Jim Traub. My continuous gratitude to friends and family—in particular to Candice Reffe, and Kimiko Hahn—for their honest help and suggestions.

I thank the Provincetown Fine Arts Work Center, The National Endowment for the Arts, and The Writer's Room for their support in the making of these poems.

Already the World

I

THE PLAYER

At noon I watched men playing basketball.
I hung against the fence envying them,
the way they didn't look at each other
but drove the rough ball up and down court
passing it through their ready hands.
I wanted to be these men.
They were not the bodies of soft edges.
It was vertical jump and wrist, their breasts
shook tensely coming down from a shot.
It seemed that nothing in the city loved a woman,
even the street where steam
rose through the black grates lifting up my skirt.

There's not much more from those months.
Yellow lilies arranged in Mason jars,
when the petals unhinged and fell—
little rafts on the furniture.
I lay around in front of a rotating fan, listening
to a woman close by practicing her opera scales.
Italian songs twisted in air currents through my room.

All around me the buildings were fat with women
singing about love or saying nothing for days.
I cared nothing for *Traviata* or *Don Giovanni*.
I wanted only to be a player
with a disciplined body;
to pass the ball like a globe,
easily and without looking,
dunking that round world, hoop after hoop,
with no other ambition than to move.

TALKING ANGEL

It was an American Bluebird—painted turquoise, racks for backpacks, hash rolled with tobacco. It got stuck overnight at the Swiss border. She says she watched an Australian woman fuck the bus driver. It is my roommate's story from her trip across Europe. I keep asking her to tell it to me. She says the driver said something over and over. The seats, covered in green plastic, made a damp popping noise. A word starting with the letter D. Tonight I tell her he was cooing *Mon Dieu*, though other nights it has been *doucement* or *diable*. Last time they were sitting up. She was crouched above him. Now he is kneeling, her back to him, an outline of moisture where her hands press on the window. Her brother is on the bus asking questions. "Where is the food?" "Where is the extra blanket?" At dawn the bus continues to Athens. They all get off. Now my roommate wants to tell me what else she saw. It is all monument and historic event. I say, "The popping noise, that's the Australian girl." If months later the girl tried to lift the driver's face up to the face of her imagination, I could not say. And could I say if later the brother and sister spoke of the night or could never speak of the night? I want to know who my roommate would be if she could be any of them. "But I was there," she says. I tell her I am the girl. I am her shadow flung across other seats. I am that girl talking angel. She is talking angel rising, blue wing net, angel updraft, wing beat. He says this time in slow American, "Damn baby, that's nice." My roommate says, "One more time. And then that's that. There was snow. That was why we waited out the night." "By the end," I say, "it wasn't really sticking, just flurries settling on the window sashes. The driver could have continued." Think of the shushing sound that cars make, tires passing over snow, yellow light from headbeams slicing through the bus. Think of the light slipping over the spent couple. That is something, don't you think? To wake for a second, see a thing all lit up. What was it? Whatever it was, now it is everything.

4

SOME CRAZY DANCING

I think I must have spent great chunks of those years
watching the girls and boys on American Bandstand,
the frug and the boogaloo shaking through their furious bodies.
I stood by the TV and danced along. I wish
I could say I was another girl, that my stories were those
of the girl who walked off-set, leading a boy—his license
snug in a back pocket—into shadow. I wish I could say
I was the girl who knew what to do with her tongue.
What I wanted in those years was mostly everything:
The neatly belted torsos, the girl's high tits,
all the worn places on the guy's jeans.
What I wanted was not to have to do one thing.
And in front of that TV as I shimmied, ponied and posed,
one afternoon I heard a man's voice somewhere close by saying
—and this I remember exactly—*Fuck me, fuck baby, do me.*
Of course the voice was inside me. Not hard to imagine why,
but harder to imagine how my own indecency undid me.
I flipped the channel, then shut it off and went out
into a nest of suburban streets; walking past landscaped
lawns, shaped bushes, cut-back flowering trees, the slate
front walks up to doors where anyone might emerge.
I know I believed it was finite:
the universe of sex moving inside me,
stars burning out, streaking through the sky, and me—
too afraid to look up or down. Under a neighbor's dogwood,
under the excitement of petals, I waited for that
insistent voice inside to step out and show me what was what.
I can't help it, it seems sweet now—desire—
can I even call it that?—more a demand,
like Dick Clark calling out some latest dance craze,
some new-fangled routine that you'd believe
might be the season's best.

PRESS

It was the summer of Son of Sam
and we girls wore our hair in ponytails.
We formed a club, our code names
the names of his girls, clipped
their reprinted photos, learned
to twist a shoulder forward.
Nights, we rode with stoned boys, impatiently
led them over the browned terrain of our bodies.
In the dark of their fathers' cars
our untanned places glowed a milky white.
When they reached inside, we arched back
in a way that would bring him to us like a howl.
We read he went for long dark hair and
in the morning we let down our ponytails.
Then August's last press of heat
sent the town to water. Boys snuck from behind
to unlatch swim suits. We dove,
our tops waving like gills. Young mothers
stayed poolside, baggy in their bodies;
the old songs off their radios were too loud.
When it was all over, it was all wrong.
We told the boys to drive us home.
There was no dog. This was no mail clerk.
We girls were oiled and brown and knew
he was out there still, aiming
to fix us forever. We would wait.
Cars came down fast off the hill.
Some never stopped for the light.

I SAID MY NAME WAS LENORE

Someone said, you've got a pretty mouth, Lenore.
The orchards, they said were pear.
A sweater, maybe a jacket. I had both.
There is nothing anyone can tell me about my mouth.
I figured the orchards were fine.
The tobacco shed was fine too.
Got me to like eggs. Anna, you're a good girl,
he'd say while he'd spoon some egg into my mouth.
Here even the sun looks different.
I came from where it was colder.
There were hinges on the shed walls.
This in the time of hundred dollar bills.
Then, I was just some girl.
Then I was not so much more myself
then a shake of untied hair.
There is nothing wrong to be called Anna.
That town was nothing to seek.
But at night you could smell them both.
The pear, the tobacco, all together.
Like in this world, they were meant best
to be smelled exactly just like that.

WATCHING LOVE

During the time I had a man and a woman
and believed I loved them both,
mostly I felt lucky.
    Sometimes after love, holding her
it was like holding a hummingbird,
some internal motion so rapid
that like wings she appeared blurred.
She'd hover in my arms
then go home to a live-in lover.
It wasn't so different for me, riding uptown
to a man with roommates who hoped I'd make him happy.

Once she asked me to strip for her.
I did it. Without music or a moon.
There were dogs in the hallway and elevator doors.
    And because she wanted to hurt me,
or because it was true,
she said I did the getting dressed better.
Afterwards we walked to where she disappeared
into the geography of subway sounds.
I waited, half believing the old trick—
a bird stuffed in, a rabbit yanked out.

I waited for what would emerge,
rising up the stairs to me.
The truth is I wanted transformation,
for anyone's love to change me beyond myself,
like waking to the miracle of ice—
coated phone wires, roads slicked,
branches weighted to the snapping—
and the world suddenly dangerous,
at risk and beautiful.

In fact it had stormed all day.
There were teenagers snowballing cars,
sliding, throwing each other down, falling
as if the snow could spare them everything.
Watching two men in winter coats
stop walking and begin to kiss,
        I thought how I might have done it over.
Left a sock on. Spoken to myself as if she wasn't there.
I watched the men move off the street,
move beyond the ragged air, into the universe of mouths.
And what was left was only their burden
of arms and legs and clunky boots,
which looked as permanent as anything I had seen.

I see now it was already changing.
The danger is that from this distance
I could make it all seem easy.
As if that night I knew to ask
who has wanted release from her own life
and heard my name unleashed inside like driving rain,
or understood that I could continue shuttling
back and forth, claiming for myself
only the dark breath between stories.
        I only know I walked all night
through streets of melting snow.
Looking up, I saw or didn't see,
as I do tonight, this bulging moon
on its steady sufficient course.

BETWEEN NIGHT AND MORNING

We wake. Your dreaming body
full in my hands. I climb onto you

like a whelp searching out the long nipple.
You come into me like a newborn taken in

and washed in its mother's mouth. I'm child
above you. Inside me you're child. We rock

making little sounds. Our eyes still shut.
When we fall back from one another into sleep

it's not because we're finished. We let
the giving carry us toward morning.

THE PROPOSITION OF BLOSSOM

Walking to town past the rental cottages.
A list of things-to-do in the pocket
of a denim skirt short enough
to make drivers honk and call.

When the wind starts up, she stops.
The gold pollen settling on her
to make its abrupt casting.

WHAT WAS LEFT OF THE ANGEL

It's only now when you were speaking about morning hats that
I suddenly thought about the girl from who knows
how many years back and thought—now I understand—
it was a *mourning* hat.
God knows, I probably have it all wrong.
And not just about the hat. "It is not right,"
that's what the girl kept saying and the boy,
I think he said it too. At least
that's what I thought they were saying.
Of course, in French. In fact, in French Canadian French,
which only, God knows, made matters worse.
Quelle plume, I wanted to say. But wound up saying something
like, *C'est une chapeau* and even
that with worrying over the *une* or *un* of it.
They were with me because that is how
it was back then. I was the one with the biggish place.
I would come back and find a girl sitting on my bed
with a plate of buttered toast. We drank wine
left from a Chilean who had gone on to Switzerland.
Luy, that was his name, the boy, not the Chilean,
and it was pronounced like Louie and her name
I'll think of it—it's right there—a French name too.
The child's name I remember. It took me
a while to figure it out. They kept saying "Didiet,"
like a kind of punctuation. "Didiet" they would say.
They kept going out and coming back with shopping bags.
She bought a pink hat. And then another—this one
with a feather. He bought colored pencils, a chocolate angel.
More wine. I came to understand they had lost the child,
this Didiet. That it was a window. They stayed three nights.
I lived alone then or with whomever, friends' friends passing
through, for some time with a Salvadoran boy, and that Chilean
who sent a postcard from Biarritz and another from Nepal.
I gave them my bed. During the night I heard them, the girl

and the boy—or really, just the girl—
her crying in my bed, her crying that grammar
I had come to understand was the child.
I remember how it sounded so French, her crying,
and how I worried that if I fell asleep she would step
out my window. He offered me a piece of the chocolate angel.
I am sure there was more wine. Even, perhaps, another hat.
Exactly what happened to the child, I never was sure, though
Luy and Anise—that was the girl's name, Anise, I knew
I'd remember—they told me and told me more than once
in those three days. There was the problem of the French.
They left in the morning. By evening I had finished off
what was left of the angel. I heard from them sometime—
a few years later. They had a new baby.
A girl, a boy, I can't remember. When she kissed me goodbye,
she was wearing that hat. They had so many packages to carry.
With all the everything going on, at some point
the dyed orange feather fell from the hat, floating
to my floor where it stayed until I swept and tidied up
which I always eventually did, God knows.

THE WEIGHT

When I think of those weeks
after my mother's death,
it is mostly of him waiting
on the mattress when I came back
from working the double shift.
Lying over him in pumps and nylons and skirt.
I can't remember ever wanting
so to be wanted.
Any way he wanted.
After, he would carry me through the bare rooms.
My big body up in his arms.
I shredded the nylons while he slept.
I made long ladders that started at my feet
and left him the flesh-tinted threads
in a nest at his head.
Then I left.
That is what I wanted most of all.

TO KNOW IN THIS BODY

These are my wood nights.
Night of pine sleep,
Night of big animal dark,
Black of ground leaf.
Lake black, the last light
Pulled down to loon darkness.
Darkness of lake wind,
Darkness of leaf rustle,
Rustle of wind. Branch
Crack, limb snap, snap
Of smallest twig.
Flush of wing. And how many times
Have I waked, clenched,
Dreading this smallest patch
Of wild? Everything
Outside and in, what
Is and isn't
Near. Fearing,
I wait for them.
Sharp wet nose.
Pointed face.
Beady eyes.
That fast coyote heart.

ON THE TABLE

After my mother's first stroke,
it was not her aimless limp through the house
that I hated most, but her arm
bent at the elbow, lifted like a waitress's arm,
the hand flattened and ready for the tray.
This mother who could not manage the knife and fork.
This mother, whom could she serve?
I noted everything
she could and could not do.
I had become the most exquisite of gourmets,
dining at a three-star restaurant
that had lost one star.
The waitress's unnetted hair, botched lipstick,
her vague floating wrist
cost me my appetite. I left without
putting one coin on the table; I left saying
close this joint, shut it down.

BEHOLD

This time it is Nana kneeling to curse
Joseph in his plot somewhere out
in God-only-knows-where Queens, where Nana
and my uncle and I have taken three hours
to get out to where my uncle said he'd get us
in less than an hour. Nana holds
her little trowel, her digging
a place for the flowers she has brought,
digging and cursing and pointing the trowel
at me, saying, "So Mrs. Big Shot, it was so important
you had to miss this beauty," and my uncle, too,
who wanders among the better graves
proclaiming that he's going to hire someone
to keep a little something nice growing all year,
whereas, I am still trying to make sense of the motel
where I stopped for directions and the toilet
I used in a room where sheets were piled
in the bathtub and someone's urine
was still foamy on the toilet seat.
        I am trying to forget the guilt
I felt coming out of that undone room
as if I had just left a difficult lover
over the Long Island Expressway, and wondering
who else by now has cleaned or sat on that toilet.
She is digging furiously with her cramped
arthritic hands, scolding the earth for denying her
a place, and in her fury she has kicked
off her old high heels and her stockinged toes—
they cannot help it—waggle pleasurably
in the good spring air.
        Up on the hills they are at work—
Puerto Ricans, I guess—mowing grass
and taking long breaks to smoke

and stub out cigarettes. They are whirring,
a wake of cuttings spitting out behind them.
        Why after all misdirection I follow Uncle's
instruction to take a quick turn and turn
the wheel into a sharp jutting pipe, is something
I chalk up to the relief of getting us back into the car,
but why the tire blows out in front of a funeral
is, for all I can guess, an act of Grandpa Joseph and God
making another bit of *tsouris* for a wife
old enough to be his mother. They turn, mourners, grievers,
looking for any distraction beyond grief or family.
We roll past, our tire flapping,
and I hear through the open window the rabbi
saying, "Yea though I walk through the valley
of the shadow of death," with his mouth hanging
crookedly on the "the" and the "of." The Puerto Ricans
hover above, ready with big shovels,
eager to go home to whomever is their home.
        Oh *mira, mira.* Oh Joseph,
here is Nana, ninety-five, blind and riding
the city buses, here is your son
living with Nana who, blind or not, washes
and presses his underpants by hand, here am I
loosening these lugs and putting on a spare
to ride fast as I can out of Queens.
        Behold the grief of expressway lovers
and the curious happiness of mourners
itchy with spring. Here comes the dirt
and the traffic-smeary sundown. Here comes
the man who fixes my tire. He admires
the puncture. It is a quick patch
which he does telling me the whole time
about the new radials, their tread,
even their longevity a thing, he says,
above all things worthy to behold.

II

TALK THE BIG HAND DOWN

1.

Angel spoke the word. Angel
had it all over the rest of us.
Better than Nimble or Quick,
Angel didn't bother jumping.
Sat on the end of the wick
and burned. People were busy,
all the hoopla of begetting.
Angel said, *Oh,* and *Oh.*
Everyone shut up fast.
      Thus, there was Oh.

Bolt screwed off the hydrant,
here were streets of annointing,
heads and toes, head to toe,
till there was looseness in every joint.

Sinner, whose feet don't stink sometimes?

Angel shook, shaking bangles strung
with silver fish, soup cans, towers.
One look said this wasn't just another
piss-ass kid looking for rapture.
Gun jacked at your temple, Angel
said, *The days of your life are numbered.*
Face it, this was revelation.

Angel said, *Say, ah, say ah.*
Say, half the time I'm lucky.
Say, I'm a mean motherfucker,
a brotherfucker, a mother brother.
Angel said, *Talk the big hand down,*
bright spot of flesh.

Talk slant river current, wind
coasted up Avenue. Talk Praise.
Talk rat off the third rail.
Ah, say ah.

Kids chopping down the street, looking
for what good comes of nothing.
Angel cuts past. What about wings?
Were there wings to remember
Great beatings? Membranous?
A stubbed something?
Who is singing *mercy, mercy now?*
Just lullabies from one wacked grandma
to a restless son. Just a song
heard through an open window.
Beets in a bowl on another old lady's lap.
Just someone's son on his knees
saying, Mama, I swear. I swear it.
Hands stained red—*that color can't be real!*—
I swear it, Mama, I saw Angel
dancing on the head
of a pin.

2.

Another promise, another boy,
some hickory dickory no good dock where
kids sat dangle-footed and ready to fall in.
What was the time? Time was there was no place
you did not hear a story of someone dancing high
and dusted and tumbling down. Into water
if you were lucky or the luckless way—
a rock, a roof, or the way they hear some kid went—
his papa left screaming, "No, that's my boy,"
when the men came to wash the street down.

3.
A whush. A wing?
Forget Angel.
Do not look back.

CALLING BROTHER

After the night you told me,
I kept thinking I saw your brother,
kept following men in our city
down streets into happy-hour bars,
recognizing a man I would never meet.
And each time that I spotted your brother
I thought how I would bring him to you
and you would have to take back
the word *suicide* and take back the word *dead.*
I thought how you would take back the six weeks
of walking the Bowery, walking
the rotten transient hallways, knocking on doors;
you would take back the shelters
where you stared into the exhausted faces of men
who go out to find jobs in a country
that will cost a poor man his life,
and the yellow faces of men who drink, get sick and drink;
you would take back wandering through
uptown clubs where white boys on heroin
snapped their fingers slowly and off-beat,
and downtown clubs where powdered girls
pressed you whispering expensive mantras;
you would take back walking the seven bridges into our city;
and take back the calls to every state—
to kids from grade school or the ones from college,
to state hospitals, to hostels and to cops.
You would take back your hate for cops.
You would stop hating the cop who said it's a guy's right
to take off and get himself good and lost,
the cop you spoke to when you woke up,
the cop you spoke to like a prayer before sleep,
the cop who six weeks later
said they'd buried your brother in Potter's Field

twelve hours after you called him in missing,
the cop who said paperwork error,
the cop who showed you photos
of a swollen body they'd pulled from the river
and the one who said that was Ricky.
I thought how you would take back the nights
you call me Ricky and I answer yes,
because a boy who grows up with his brother in the same room
needs sometimes to call out in the dark and hear a reply.
I thought that sooner or later I would find him,
a man who—like all of us—one day wakes up,
puts on his clothes, locks the door, stumbles out
into the bright spotlight of the living,
goes down to the river wanting to fall in,
wants—even if by accident—the shocking wet
of something clear that gives,
but—as much by accident—looks up and keeps going.
I thought how I wanted to bring your brother back
and stand him before you.
You would say his name and he would answer yes.
You would take back the word and take back the word,
look up, say yes and get on with this living.

MAYBE THERE IS NOTHING
SPECIAL GOING ON

Maybe there is nothing special going on.
We are reading or we are eating supper,

Maybe we are driving a back road. I look over
and see that if I stopped the car and got out,

if I started dancing and singing on the loose dirt,
if I put down the book and held your face in my hands,

or pressed myself to you, it would not matter,
You are too far from me.

Grief—I've seen her at night;
the way she dresses up, my god, she sparkles,

she shimmers. I can't blame you. I'd go to her too.
Who wouldn't want her and then want her again

once they'd felt all the ways
she makes a body shake.

FOOD

At first there is no blood. At first
there is only the blessed, born naked and blind,
six months fatted on hand-picked grasses, rabbit
that Juan Del Peral is grateful is stupid
like all rabbits and easily lulled into feeling
the plucking of its ears a sign to relax.
Because Juan Del Peral wants to be an honest man,
he picks up the rabbit by its hind legs—
letting its slack body hang—pats it across
the head, pulls the ears until they fall
close to the skull and never turns away
from the others. Let them see, he thinks,
that the man who cleans their cages and sings
to them his best love songs, will strike them down
with not too much effort and less regret. It is true, too,
that the hand that comes down on the soft place
where the ears and neck meet is quick and light,
a lighter hand, for instance, than a man might use
on the body of an erring child. But about regret,
Juan Del Peral is only partways true.
With the rabbit hung to be bled, he sits back
to wet the skinning blade. The rabbits seem jittery.
He thinks how he has watched their twitchy sleep, and how
he has opened a rabbit, held the testicles in his palm before
dropping them in the bucket, how he has pinched
and then pulled back their skin, yanking and
yanking until he wonders if this time
it is his own skin that will go, and how he has bled
the necks, catching the first blood to save for cooking. There,
there, he says to his rabbits,
though he knows that one by stupid one
with short pulls he will convince them of his love
until the ears relax and with a skilled soft rap
he will strike the next beauty down.

AT NOON IN TORRE BARRO

Between birds and cats there is no grief. Only repetition.
And later the birds are still at it, fisting their bodies down,
dive-bombing street cats that nobody
in town admits she feeds. Now a mongrel bitch wanders up
the scarp, the scab-headed cats gathering under stairs
to leap at her like they are the big dogs.
The bitch seems barely to notice, cutting through alleys
and small plots matted with vegetables.
Garlic. Out of every open window, from deep
within the houses' guts breaks the open cut of garlic.
And what is not happening here
is as easy to guess as what happens.
The mongrel bitch skits out, sliding on loose rock,
her legs bent like something already snapped.
Inside a woman kneels on crocheted doilies
she will wash at night. The birds make their *soweet soweets*
and their *tacaw tacaws*. It is no longer, of course,
exactly noon. Boys find each other at the bottom
where the hill breaks down quickly into rock and dust.
Because they can, the boys darken rocks with piss,
spit at slow flies. Stones chucked hit boxes and cans
that blow off in another day's wind.
The mongrel bitch licks at herself.
Let's go, says the older boy but no one goes.
The woman shifts on her bony knees, reciting
the seven works of mercy. There is time for the seven wonders
and then for the seven deadly sins. When he says again,
Let's go, the boys start up, quietly,
single file, each leaning inescapably into each step.

HOW THE FIRST GENERATION LEARNS

When the family revolves through the door
at the Idlewild Airport, it is 1963.

I am placed on a plastic chair,
the luggage a tight barricade around me.

I have never been on vacation and I don't want to go.
No one tells me what's happening

when our father walks off
saying, *Be quiet. Don't say a word.*

Now we are just another grainy photograph.
The dark mother with three dark daughters.

The December wool coats. Suitcase.
I watch him approach the ticket counter

and when he's there, I know what is to be known.
Immigrant sweat a sickly sheen

above his lip, a white
sour taste in his mouth,

fingers knitted behind his back.
It's as though anything might happen.

It's as though the young male employee
of a major commercial airline

is the border guard and our tickets
are papers for which there will be bribe.

I want to touch Father's nervous hands,
pull him back and go home. No one

has to tell me what's happening.
I've listened to him say it would be like this.

I've seen the photographs where they are like us,
the one where children remain with one parent,

the ones where the dirt is freshly turned
and there is no one.

SURVIVOR

After textiles my father worked in futures.
He put away the squares of silk and cotton,
taught himself to buy and sell
a thing and never see it.
All abstraction and then the dollar.
Every morning, he bit the lucky silver head.
He kept coins in dresser drawers,
suitcase of currency.

For him the world was a map
of circumstance and the Jew:
bullish and bearish
were only stalling tactics
until a new border guard.

When his wife died a natural death
my father could not cry like one
who entering the beloved temple
sees the arc curtain torn away,
the Torah gone.
My father wept the bewildered tears
of one who had resolved
that even in a crashing market
there was always a future
to be bought back.

THE PRESIDENTIAL DEBATE

Last night after watching the candidates debate—
their paired cameos, their accusations
of debt and deficit—I stood at my window.
Lifting it, I hoped to hear some fevered sounds,
the diligent practice of pleasure. I wanted
a private cry to pull me from my national loneliness
into insurgence, ecstatic and patriotic.

I was certain that somewhere above the mesh of streets
a man opened the back buttons of a woman's blouse
and reached under her arms to balance
a breast in each hand. She turned her face
and found him unexpectedly profiled in the mirror.
Now, she said and watched her own hand
guiding his fingers till they opened inside her.

Last night I went and stood at my window.
The dark buildings rose against the dark sky.
The moon was fastened at the throat of the city.

NOT THE WHOLE STORY

That I am the one left to tell this story
is neither a coin in the overflowing cup of Injustice
nor the gold star on a report handed back
to the proud second grader—
it's just the dumb luck of the living.
Truth is, that you could have told it better
doesn't matter anymore, or that who am I?
friend of a friend, one who laughed at some jokes,
gave you a lift from a beach wedding,
held your hand not that often
in the five years of your dying.
Or maybe not. The story is simple.
You had it wrong. The secret is not
that a man likes to run a dry razor up
over his squat gymnast muscles or
press-on-nail by press-on-nail sculpt a woman's hand
that later will stroke a cunt or cock. Or close
the bar tapping at the smoothed brass railing.
The secrets are never so simple and simpler,
the way, for instance, today I stalked a man
for ten blocks, watched your small, squared frame jaunting
ahead until at the 18th Street crosswalk,
I'm in step with a man grown suddenly gangly and tall.
Or that waking this morning I looked at Jim asleep
and thought, *my face is sleeping.*
I hear a man call your name, but he asks for Sandy.
The man I thought was you carried tulips wrapped in plastic.
Jim woke, rolled over saying, "There's something
I've got to tell you." I lay back
on a pillow, ready for nothing. "Tell me
the whole story," I said. "Tell me every last thing."

III

THIRD MONTH

At first you were in the mouth,
nausea uncalmable.
Or you were the hard stools of constipation.
At night rocked
over to sleep at a child's hour,
I slept with pillows layered
to ease my swollen breasts.
In books they claimed you were
no bigger than a fingernail,
but I could feel you, gargantuan,
settling in my body, assuming
what you needed to live,
risking everything
even if it meant risking
mother love.

BREAKING THE AIR

Now that you are here among us,
I can see how it will happen.
I watch pretty wives calling out
to their husbands but saying Daddy.
And the men spent with new exhaustion.

I look and already he is less a lover
than a father, prepared to spring up
for any disaster. Already
he touches me with too much respect.

When we go out, they are everywhere,
adorable and hungry.
While the mothers and fathers talk,
they wheel toward the curb.

On the playground we watch the older ones
swing dangerously, feet first breaking the air,
and I feel you, already hatching a plan,
where, pumping higher and harder, higher and
harder, you jump out at us and we must fall
to catch you with all available hands.

NINTH MONTH

Already you are moving down.

Already your floating head
engaged in the inlet
from where you will head out.

Already the world, the world.

And you are slipping
down, away from my heart.

WHERE IT WOULD LAND

Yet the other leg steps back,
away from the world.
As if it were possible to swing
away from the solid.
As if approaching this world
the baby saw where it would land
and struggled to be gone.

AT WAR

It is already hot at seven-thirty
in the morning when the women stand
with wet bundles.
        The stubborn laundry
        will not shake open as they hang it out.
The shirts don't want
        to retake shape in the air,
showing the possibility of a boy's heart.
        Keeping themselves crouched,
the cotton pants know the slightest
movement could be noticed.
        The socks are tongues
which want to say nothing
of a foot's particular shape
        walking at night.
The women also have fear
and tell this to the clothes on the line.
        There isn't one who doesn't know
        a mother's terrible story.
But the women have no patience left
and tell the clothes to be practical.
        They want to stuff
every pocket and seam with strong yellow sun
        to be tossed out
like blinding grenades,
        protecting the daughters and sons.

ROOTING

In the first days it was not
the new one who amazed me
so much as the ones who lumbered
up our stairs and settled
their weighted bodies down.
I saw them as they had been.
Swaddled. Eyes cottoned free of mucus.
Gas patted from their stomachs.
Saw their hungry rooting,
their not-yet-of-this-world smiles.
I watched them grow dizzy
looking at the new one,
as if they had just looked out
off a high cliff, past the uneven rocks,
the fallen piles of scree.
At the bottom a sea of mothers sang,
Jump. Jump to mama, baby, Jump.

PSALM

All night pacing.
The baby hanging off my tit.
He has been at it for hours.
Four to be exact.
My one with eyes open
cannot cast himself
out into his blue sleep.
In the darkness singing,
in the darkness singing,
my off-pitched voice
trying every note
to save us both.

He got himself ready on the bed.

He watched her wave a slim tube in the air. Just for us, she said.
She knelt over him. They said be prepared, she said.

He closed his eyes.

Like a new virgin, she said. He pulled her head down, running
his teeth inside of her lips, biting along the just wet inside
ridge. He sucked her lips into a tight clasp inside of his mouth.
Pulling off his face, she cocked her head, angling toward some
unavoidable sound.

He opened one eye.

Oh, sweet bleeding mother of Jesus, here it comes, she said,
while the first white drops dropped from her breasts, then
dropping faster till they pooled on the man's soft stomach.

THE WAY HAGAR TELLS IT

And Sarai said to Abram, "Behold now,
the Lord has prevented me from bearing
children; go into my maid; it may be
that I shall obtain children from her."
                                    —*Genesis 16*

1 · THE AGREEMENT

My door left open. His brief cry
and Sarai saying, *Now come home, Husband.*
Then their feet on the packed dirt.
A thin wind breaking in the brush.
To be given this way, fetched,
readied, a she-goat.

Days later, passing I smile,
take him down among the wet reeds
say, *Watch*, dancing wildly
until he became insistent.
When she calls he is singing
a nonsense song about the lizard
bathing on the mountain top.

What they took, I myself take.
Can I be more blamed?

At night the mistress comes to my bed.
She holds her hand on my fullness
and says, *My baby.* She presses
the nipple for the early milkish fluid,
and reaches her hand to measure my sex.
I think they will take everything.
The man. The woman. *Be quick, be fierce!*
I say to the fourth heart that beats inside me.

My boy sits in the mud
sifting, clumping, building.
Oh, my Egypt. He calls,
Watch, watch,
and I see this slave's son
run in circles toppling
markets and nations.

The man coming home
crosses the yard,
stopping to kiss his son.
Now our males holding each other
over fallen houses.

I take long strokes
with the comb through my mistress's hair.

Now it is her two hands
folded on a belly.
As if she will be the first woman
to squat down
and spit out a child!
As if everyone had to gather
her unfilled folds of common cloth.

I hear everything in the forest,
the rush of leaves, the scatter of bugs.
So when the angel speaks
it is just one more sound.
The angel says, *Nation*, and opens the well.

AND NOT SO MUCH READY

And not so much ready
  as already

through the door with the child
  saying, ma ma ma ma,

and this mother body
  come on her.

Dishes, even after
  she has finished the dishes,

there are dishes
  in the sink.

Now the child is in the corner
  doing his dance of *No.*

This is the love song.
  The lullabye.

A message to stuff
  in the craw of the bird

that wastes an afternoon in the elm
  and then flies away.

THE CROWNING

Then they could see you.

The small dark crown posed
in the chamber, the red mantle
still wrapped around you.

Here! Out here! they shouted,
listening for your broken cry, delighting
in your first spectacle of weakness.

MILK

That first winter coming back to our bed what did I want?
My mother tits tongued, licked back to breasts again?
Can I say that sometimes it came on me, a pleasure
in that dark where I rocked, taking the clamp
of the baby's bony ridged gums. How I came back
to our bed one breast overfull and leaking,
the baby fallen off the nipple and into sleep.
I have still not said it—not just pleasure—
a pulse in the cunt in the dark while the baby sucked.
How you slept through the nights. How I wanted that too,
to walk the corridor back and forth between your breath
and the baby's hunger. How it was less walking
than it was prowling, curling around myself
and waking to find myself in different rooms.
How every room that winter was a kind of leaving.
A duct engorged or cracked, without even pleasure sometimes,
a growth spurt so that all day was a frenzy of milk.
I would waste the extra milk into the bathroom sink.
I would look up to see myself in a spray of milk —
some she-beast ready to kill for or kill her young,
or I would not look at myself at all, walking
back through rooms we did not have, waking in moss fields
waking on avenues, sitting on dented car hoods to nurse.
And what of it? What of wanting? What of milk
and the bleaty hunger of this baby and that baby
who have long left the tit? And what of avenues?
What now to say to Jen, who calls
to say she is having the baby no one thinks she should have.
She says she wants to have it and give it up.
I tell her how up in those other days Dick cooked
and ate his wife's after-birth. I was not looking for that.
I was looking for a way back.

I was looking for the mossy tongue.
What of that bed we left there, taking with us
only the idea of the bed, sides we call yours and mine?
I could show you how, even now, I can roll a nipple
and thin drops of clear yellow milky fluid bead
in the folds. I could show you this. Or I could,
as I do, lick it off my finger and it is done.

EVERYDAY

This morning
outside the only early morning
cafe in this till-all-hours coastal town,
      a man said:
                  Thank you for this brief encounter,
which was mostly him warning that knocking
up against too many tourists zaps power;
                  but,
            how, anyhow,
each weekend he's down from Manchester.
That, and me saying: Excuse me,
      to chase my reeling
         eighteen month old back into the cafe
where booth to booth he smiled at men and women,
alone or paired, tanking coffee,
  then crooned
  at the smiles he could pull.
            His—yes, I'll say it—
brief encounters.
         One winter I lived in this town alone.

And why I want to tell this to the man and do,
is why that winter I already groomed my nostalgia,
      preening about my poorly heated bay-whipped rental
            holding back
the silvered light of early evening
by imagining how later it would glisten sad
and precious in the telling.
                  Everyday
my boy wants the same stories over and over.
He wants the same ta da ta da ta dum
of the alligator's trumpet mouth, hooray
for the pilot's lifting plane,

54

bye-bye
to the vanishing bear.
        This is what I meant—
making tedium noble in the retelling.

When he was six months old I made lists.
Flowers. Cleaning supplies. Diaper artists with kids. Toxic
plants. State capitals. More diapers.
Why was it a poet friend said: Please, no mother poems?
        When we say *forever* do we mean *for good?*
I said none of this this morning. Nor did I talk
about the vines Michaela and I hauled
from the December woods to coil for gift wreaths.
        Or how, later,
arms, face, neck all blooming wild with poison ivy
I claimed:
    But I'm immune.
It was more than once my son squirmed free.

Days ago
    after I wrote: This morning outside
the only early morning cafe, my son pulled himself,
bottle and books onto my lap and waited.

Now he and his father are off on their bicycle.
My designated hour and one half.
    A cormorant settles
on a motor boat's hull. A windsurfer
  slices past.
My boy hovers. Ta da ta dum.
                    Forever.
Somewhere they are braking down steep hills.
The magenta geraniums lean in their pots.

They stop; throw rocks at the incoming tide.
Down beach, a barking dog.
  For good. Here, someone lifting her pen.
      Hooray. Bye-bye.
   Someone shouts: I am home.

Already the World

was composed in 10/13 Minion
on a Gateway 2000 PC using PageMaker 5.0 for Windows
at The Kent State University Press;
imaged to film from PS files and printed by sheet-fed offset
on 60-pound Glatfelter Supple Opaque Natural stock
(a recycled acid-free paper),
and notch case bound into 88-point binder's boards
covered in ICG Kennett cloth,
also notch adhesive bound with paper covers
printed in two colors on 12-point C1S stock
finished with matte film lamination
by Thomson-Shore, Inc.;
designed by Will Underwood;
and published by

The Kent State University Press
KENT, OHIO 44242